GW01418040

The Europea... .... Finance Guide

An aide memoir for organisations running or planning to run ESF funded projects

by

Margaret Goddard ACMA

ICOM gratefully acknowledges the financial support of the European Social Fund which enabled it to publish this guide.

Fourth edition updated September 1998

Published by

Industrial Common Ownership Movement Limited
20 Central Road, Leeds LS1 6DE, UK

Tel 0113 2461737/8 Fax 0113 2440002
Internet/e-mail icom@icom.org.uk

ISBN 1 870018 26 5

Price £8.00

Design and production: **total** coverage

Acknowledgements

I would like to say thank you to all those individuals who gave me constructive advice on the content of the guide.

In particular I would like to thank Helen Seymour of ICOM, whose idea it was to write the guide and who gave me enormous support and corrected the punctuation.

I am very grateful to both Frank McKay of the Verification and Audit Section in the ESF Unit and Elizabeth Solowo-Coker of the ESF Unit at the Department for Education and Employment, whose suggestions have greatly improved the content of the guide.

I would also like to thank Derek Collinson of ICOM for checking the calculations and providing useful comments. Thanks also to Neil Skinner of ICOM and to Pat Collinson for their comments.

Industrial Common Ownership Movement (ICOM)

ICOM is the UK federation of democratic employee owned businesses. From 1990 to 1997 it was sector manager for applications to the European Social Fund from the co-operative and community economic development sector; it continues to represent the sector on the national Monitoring Committees for ESF Objectives 3 & 4 and is a member of the national committees for the ADAPT and EMPLOYMENT programmes.

Margaret Goddard is the European Social Fund and European Projects Financial Manager at ICOM. She is a qualified chartered management accountant with a background in training and provides training, advice and guidance on record-keeping for organisations running ESF funded projects.

Contents

Introduction

This guide has been produced in order to help organisations, particularly smaller organisations, properly administer their European Social Fund monies. It will also serve as a guide to those public bodies providing co-financing (matching funding) for ESF and who have a responsibility for monitoring those projects for which they are providing the matching monies. The guide has been produced in order to:

- indicate to those organisations not yet involved with ESF the kinds of financial systems they will need to operate if they wish to run ESF funded schemes

- assist those organisations running ESF supported schemes to improve and refine their financial systems

- aid those organisations responsible for the monitoring of ESF supported projects, ie those organisations providing matching funding for ESF.

The guide can be used as an aide memoir for organisations planning to run or running ESF funded projects. It should not be used as the definitive guide. If you have any specific queries on ESF finance you should contact your Government Office in the region for advice.

What is the European Social Fund?

The European Social Fund (ESF) is one of the three Structural Funds established under the Treaty of Rome to strengthen the economic and social cohesion of the European Community; the other two funds are the European Regional Development Fund (ERDF) and the European Agricultural Guidance and Guarantee Fund – Guidance Section (EAGGF).

The ESF aims to help improve employment opportunities in the European Union by providing financial support towards the running costs for vocational training schemes, guidance and counselling projects and job creation measures.

In Great Britain the ESF is administered by the Department for Education and Employment (DfEE) who has the responsibility for the proper expenditure of ESF monies. Community Initiatives including EMPLOYMENT and ADAPT are part of the ESF and projects run under these must follow ESF rules.

The DfEE produces a quarterly newsletter, *ESF News* which is free to ESF applicants and contains up to date details of ESF policy, technical matters, and examples of good practice. If you would like to receive the newsletter contact ICOM on telephone 0113 2461738 or fax 0113 2440002 with your contact details and these will be added to the mailing list.

From 1998 the responsibility for selection of projects for ESF Objective 3 has been devolved to Regional Committees. The arrangements for receiving applications are to be defined by Government Offices and these may be different in each region.

What are the funds to be used for?

Organisations applying for ESF monies must plan projects which fall within the broad subjects of vocational training, retraining, job creation (including self-employment opportunities) or vocational guidance and counselling.

Who can apply for ESF?

Any legally constituted organisation (not individuals) running eligible schemes and able to access financial support from a public body (e.g. local authority, Training and Enterprise Council / Local Enterprise Company, Government department, voluntary organisation).

What can be claimed?

It is important to understand that ESF is not a grant; it is a contribution towards the actual eligible costs of running a project. In general, in non Objective 1 areas, ESF contributes 45% of eligible costs. This is called the *intervention rate*.

In Objective 1 areas (in the UK these are N Ireland, Merseyside and the Highlands and Islands of Scotland) the intervention rate varies between 50% and 65% of eligible costs depending on the region.

This means that ESF project promoters must keep accurate records of their income and expenditure because income and costs relating to ESF must be easily identifiable within the organisations' books of account, i.e. records must be transparent.

How will anyone know if you don't keep accurate records or if you claim more than actual costs?

Organisations which run ESF projects may be audited at any time by one or more bodies. These include the Department for Education and Employment ESF Unit's Verification and Audit Section (VAS), the European Commission, the European Court of Auditors, the Regional Government Office, the match funders, other Government departments (Scottish Office, Welsh Office, the Department of Trade and Industry). If an audit is unsatisfactory then the ESF project promoter may be required to repay some or all of the ESF monies.

How do I apply? Do I get the money all at once? Is it easy to get ESF funding? Who decides who gets what?

Hopefully this book will answer all these questions. Basically the majority of ESF funding is for one year only or less, between January and December each year. If you are successful in gaining funding in one year that is no guarantee that you will be successful in subsequent years. However it may be possible to gain multi annual approval in some years. You complete an application form, usually before the beginning of the year in question. It goes through a selection process and if successful will be recommended for funding. First and second advance payments of 50% and 30% of the ESF approved amount will be made during the year but these may be subject to delays. After the end of the ESF year you complete a final claim form which details the actual outcomes of the project including the actual expenditure. The final payment is the balance of ESF due, based on the final claim figures. It is paid approximately 12 months *after* the end of the year in which the project is run.

Section 1 Applying for ESF – the basics

Who do I apply to?

The process of applying for ESF monies very much depends on which Objective you are applying under for mainstream ESF, or under which of the Community Initiatives you are proposing to apply.

With effect from 1998, ESF Objectives 3 and 4 operate on a regional basis, with each region having an allocation of monies. In each region there is a Regional Committee which is responsible for doing the selection of eligible projects. Certain other administrative and support functions are the responsibility of Government Offices in the region although the functions may be devolved to independent secretariats in some regions.

ESF Objectives 1, 2, and 5b operate through regional committees, with the secretariat being provided by a Regional Government Office. The committee is made up of representatives from the region and they put together the selection criteria for ESF. For Objectives 1, 2 and 5b you apply direct to the relevant regional secretariat or through a local partnership.

Some of the Community Initiatives, such as RECHAR and RENAVAL are also operated on a regional basis, often by the same committee that manages the ESF Objective 2 in the area and so you would apply direct to the regional secretariat. Other Community Initiatives such as EMPLOYMENT are operated on a national basis, with representatives from the sectors and other expert groups forming committees to decide on the selection criteria.

Contact your Government Office or the Department for Education and Employment's (DfEE) ESF Unit in London for further advice on how to apply.

Co-financing or match funding

ESF will not provide all the funding necessary for your project. Indeed, in order for you to be considered for ESF funding, you must already have some funding in place. This is called co-financing or match funding. ESF will contribute a fixed percentage to eligible costs. This percentage is called the intervention rate. The rate is an average of 45% for ESF in non Objective 1 areas.

The average intervention rate for ESF in Objective 1 areas is 65%.

See Section 2 for more information on match funding.

Eligible expenditure

ESF eligible expenditure is detailed in the guidance notes for Objective 3 ESF issued by the DfEE. It is divided into three categories:

Staff costs

Beneficiary costs

Other costs.

1. Staff costs – the following costs are eligible:
You can include the salary and wage costs of staff employed by your organisation plus employer's National Insurance Contributions and pension costs. Staff can include trainers, counsellors, managers, admin staff. Costs of external staff can also be claimed. With effect from 1998, volunteer time can also be included see Section 3 for further details.

Travel and subsistence costs for staff and the costs of external training courses for staff can also be claimed where these relate to the project.

2. Beneficiary costs – the following are eligible:
You can include the costs of wages or a daily/weekly allowance paid to beneficiaries with National Insurance and pension where applicable. Beneficiary daily travel costs and travel, board and lodging for external courses and costs of childcare can be claimed.

Where you are paying for childcare (or other dependant care) rather than providing an in-house nursery or crèche, you claim the costs under this heading. For example, you may be planning to pay child minders or after-school clubs.

3. Other costs - the following are eligible

You can include the rent and/or costs of leasing of buildings and the hire and lease of equipment. However only certain lease costs are eligible (see Section 5 for more detail).You can include the depreciation costs of owned equipment - these must be real costs to the organisation (see Section 5 for more detail). Cleaning, minor repairs and maintenance are eligible, as are rates, water rates, insurance, gas and electricity costs.

Purchase of consumables, of basic office furnishings and the purchase of **new** small items of equipment to a maximum value of £350 per item are eligible.The costs of providing aids and **minor** adaptations of premises and equipment where the project will include people with disabilities, for example ramps, and adaptations to toilets and computers can be included.

The costs of external training courses for beneficiaries, for example, college costs, first aid course are eligible. However, make sure that you negotiate a reasonable price as college charge-out rates often include a hefty profit element.

Advertising of training courses, general documentation and administration costs incurred in support of ESF activity and evaluation costs are eligible.You can include the costs of stationery, postage and telephone.

Running costs of any nursery provision and or running costs of care of other dependants provided in-house and where beneficiaries are not required to contribute to the costs are claimed under the heading of "other costs".

You can include the costs of audit, as well as legal and accountancy service where these are used for the ESF project. For transnational projects you are able to claim translation and interpreting costs.

Eligible costs may differ for the different funds and in subsequent years, so it is vital that you check the current relevant guidance for the fund you are planning to apply under.

Ineligible expenditure

There are some costs that you cannot claim under an ESF project. These are bank charges, loan interest, overdraft interest and other financial charges.Consultancy fees are ineligible, including any person or organisation you pay as a consultant to complete your ESF application and/or final claim forms. However, you can pay external trainers or outside evaluators.

You cannot claim for non-statutory allowances paid to staff, including such things as commissions and profit sharing schemes.

The purchase of depreciable equipment and buildings is ineligible, i.e. you can't claim for capital expenditure. However, you can claim the depreciation costs of owned equipment, and remember you can buy new (i.e. not second hand) individual items of equipment up to a limit of £350 cost per item.

See Appendix 1 for a list of eligible and ineligible costs for Objective 3 for 1999.

Subcontracting the training and/or running projects in partnership with other organisations

The organisation that is the ESF applicant may not always be the one actually delivering all of the project. The applicant may be subcontracting most or all of the work to another organisation. Or, the project delivery may be shared between a number of partners, with one partner being the ESF applicant. In both of these cases the applicant organisation is still wholly responsible for all aspects of the project; they must make sure that there are clear records and audit trails in place within the subcontracting organisation and/or other partner organisations. **The subcontractors and partners must show the true level of costs i.e. that they are only claiming ESF eligible expenditure.** According to ESF rules it is the ESF applicant that is responsible for refunding any ESF monies if things go wrong , even if it is the subcontractor or a partner that was responsible for not complying with ESF regulations. Thus you must make sure that you have clear contracts and/or partnership agreements in place and that there is regular monitoring of subcontractors'/partners' financial and general records.

Section 2 Applying for ESF – the application

Putting the application budget together

This is the first stage of the financial management of your project. It requires time and thought to the needs of the organisation, the beneficiaries and those who will be delivering the training. Remember if you are successful with your application for ESF funding, you will be expected to run the project as stated in the application at the cost as stated. Once you have received approval for ESF for your project, you cannot then expect to get more money if you over spend. You can receive less ESF than the amount approved, but not more.

The budget needs to be as realistic as possible. Start by looking at the outline training plan and the list of eligible costs. You also need to consider the selection criteria for the particular fund you are applying under. For example, it may be that, in order to gain points in the selection criteria you need to include costs of beneficiaries' travel and childcare\dependant care costs; you may need to include costs of offering accredited courses to beneficiaries. Thoroughly research all costs. Some types of costs are particularly difficult to estimate, in particular childcare costs. However you need to try and make sure you include reasonably realistic estimates based on past experience within your organisation, or talk to people within similar organisations who have provided childcare for beneficiaries.

Take care to include all of the budget lines you are likely to need. You can add budget lines after the application has been submitted and approved but you will need to get written approval as it is considered to be a significant change to the application. You should obtain written approval from the relevant secretariat for any significant changes. (See Section 4 for further details of significant changes).

Remember, once you have received approval for a specific amount of ESF monies for a particular project, it is not possible for you to receive more than that approved amount for that project.

Getting down to detail

When you apply for ESF and Community Initiatives monies, you will develop one or more project ideas. It is possible to combine similar project ideas into one ESF project. For example, you may wish to train unemployed people in care skills, information technology skills and painting and decorating skills; you are offering full NVQs, guidance and counselling, job search skills and literacy/numeracy training if required. If the courses were a similar length and you wished to offer tasters and a choice of skills to beneficiaries, then you could design one project to include all three main skill areas. However, if the project becomes too convoluted, it may be that it becomes difficult to understand what you are trying to achieve, and your project may be rejected. So try and develop coherent and/or separable project ideas.

When you apply for ESF and Community Initiatives you complete a form for each project. Each project has to include the following information as a minimum:

- The purpose of the project and the objectives you are setting out to achieve. Take care not to confuse the project objectives with project aims. Project objectives should be specific, measurable, achievable and time-bound. You must include the numbers of beneficiaries you are expecting to train and the targets in respect of outcomes, i.e. people into jobs and/or further training, numbers achieving a specific qualification. At final claim stage you will be expected to report against the project objectives as stated in the application, so you need to consider what performance criteria you are going to use in order to measure how successful you have been with regard to the initial objectives.

- How the project meets all of the criteria, aims and objectives relevant to the particular Operational Programme, objective and priority under which it is being submitted. This would include details of the target group of trainees, identifying their particular needs and any difficulties they face and how the project will meet those needs.

- The ESF money must be additional. This means that ESF money is there to support projects that would not otherwise have taken place. On the application form therefore you are obliged to state how the project is providing value for money. In order to determine whether the project is providing value for money, ask yourself the following questions:

  Does the project increase the quantity of training in terms of numbers of trainees and/or training hours?

  Does the project allow the provider to maintain existing projects which would otherwise be cut back due to lack of finance, or allow them to be brought forward or not to be postponed?

  Does the project produce additional outputs such as higher qualifications or more jobs?

  Is the project new and/or innovatory and could not be run using the provider's own resources?

  Does the project enable new stable jobs to be created or self employment which would not be made available without it?

  Are we certain that the project is not already fully funded by another funding source?

- Information on the relationship of the project to the needs of the labour market, identifying skill shortages or particular sectoral difficulties

- Expenditure analysis – more of this later.

- The total number of hours of activity for beneficiaries, for example if you are planning to recruit 20 beneficiaries who will be given training, guidance and/or work experience for 21 hours per week over 26 weeks, the total hours will be 10920 (20 x 21 x 26).

- The breakdown of hours per beneficiary between theory, practical, work experience and guidance and counselling.

Getting the budget together

It is probably easier to construct the budget if you categorise your expenditure into three main types. (It is not necessary to show these different categories on the application form, it is useful from the point of view of preparing the information, setting it out on the application and setting up a system for recording the actual costs).The three types of costs are:

- The project's **direct costs**, ie they are costs that are associated only with this project. Examples of these are college costs for beneficiaries or beneficiary allowances.

- Indirect costs, ie that are *shared between different ESF projects.* Examples of these are costs of an outside evaluation, consumables such as computer disks, calculators.

- Indirect costs, ie costs that are **shared with the rest of the organisation.** This will be the majority of the costs and includes most of the overheads such as rent and rates, heat, light and cleaning, administration staff.

Tackling the project's direct costs first, here are examples of these under the three types of costs, ie staff costs, beneficiary costs and other costs.

Direct costs

Staff costs:

Your project is planning to use two external trainers for the project. One will be used for half a day a week for the first 10 weeks of the training with an extra 3 days preparation time. She charges by the day. The other will be used on a sessional basis for one to one guidance and counselling and you need to make an estimate of the number of hours you will be using him. He charges by the hour.There will be 20 beneficiaries on the project. It is a 26 week course.

The detail will be shown on the application form as follows:

External trainer 0.5 days a week for 10 weeks
plus 3 days preparation time
8 days at £300 per day £2400

External trainer – counselling and guidance –
26 weeks x 20 beneficiaries at an average of 0.5 hour
per week per beneficiary x £30 per hour £7800

Beneficiary costs:

You are planning to pay all beneficiaries' travel costs and in order to do this have decided to purchase weekly travel passes. You are also planning to pay all childcare costs direct either to child minders or a local nursery. Research has shown that the ESF beneficiaries will have at least 1 child each requiring childcare. You decide to budget for more than that.

The detail will be shown on the application form as follows:

Travel for beneficiaries –
20 beneficiaries x 26 weeks x £5 per week £2600

Childcare costs for beneficiaries – 25 children x 26 weeks
at an average cost of £58 per week per child £37700

Other costs:

This is an accredited course and there are costs associated with this. Also you are planning to buy 5 cameras to enable the beneficiaries to put together a portfolio of photographs to help them to gain their accreditation. These must cost no more than £350 each.

The detail will be shown on the application form as follows:

General documentation – costs associated with gaining the qualification 20 beneficiaries at £228 each £4560

Purchase of small items of equipment (cameras – photos required for beneficiaries' portfolios) 5 cameras at £95 each £475

See Appendix 2 for more examples of direct costs.

The calculation of indirect costs can be more complicated. These are costs shared between different ESF projects and costs shared between ESF and non ESF.

Indirect costs

This is where we have to use apportionment techniques. These are very important as you will be expected to show how you apportioned costs on applications, but, more importantly, they are always examined during an audit visit. There are several different methods of apportionment.

Apportionment may be -

- based on staff time

- based on beneficiary hours

- based on the length of the course

- based on area/space used

- based on actual recorded usage.

What you cannot do:

- You *cannot* apportion costs on the basis of your organisations' turnover, ie ESF funded projects represent half of your income therefore you will claim half of the organisations' overhead costs in the ESF application.

- You *cannot* apportion costs on the basis of beneficiary numbers in different projects/courses as the hours may differ and therefore the costs.

- You should *not* use a notional figure for apportionment, eg "we reckon a charge of 70% of overheads should cover the costs". It may be wildly out, with the result that your project may not be viable (if the figure is less than a true one) or you may underspend or be required to repay some ESF monies (if the figure is more than it should be).

You can use different methods of apportionment for different types of cost. It is important to choose methods that are meaningful, at the same time taking into account how your systems will record the information needed at final claim stage.

Apportionment in more detail

1. Apportionment based on staff time.
There are different categories of staff to take into account. These are trainers and non teaching staff. The latter includes administration and finance staff, supervisory and management staff. It is the time spent on the ESF projects by the trainers and teaching staff that is the most useful figure for calculating apportionment of overheads.

However, the first thing to do is to calculate the staff costs themselves, as we can then use the information from these to calculate an overhead apportionment.

a) Trainers and teaching staff time must be recorded for ESF purposes, so these staff would be expected to keep a daily time sheet, showing what they were doing (training, guidance/ counselling, preparation, work placement visit, course administration), where they were doing it, the date and the start and finish times. These records therefore can be used as back up documentation for apportioning their time. However you will need to *estimate* the time to be spent at application stage. **NB The *actual* time spent on the project must be used for calculation of the final claim figures.**

Example I

You are planning a 420 hour course. One of the trainers will deliver 200 hours of the course. She will, in addition, require 50 hours preparation time and 10 hours course administration time. That is 260 hours. She is a full time worker for the organisation with 5 weeks annual holiday entitlement and 8 days public holidays. She works a 35 hour week (5 days a week). Her salary is £15,000 plus £1,560 Employers' National Insurance Contribution (NIC).

First calculate how many hours she works a year. The weeks worked are 52 minus 5 (annual holiday) minus 1.6 (one and three fifths weeks public holiday). This equals 45.4 weeks at work. Multiply this by 35 hours per week. This is 1589 hours at work each year. (You can adjust this for any sick leave taken at the end of the year). So the trainer's salary costs chargeable to ESF are

$$\frac{£16560}{1589 \text{ hours}} \quad \times \quad 260 \text{ hours} \quad = \quad £2,709.63$$

You don't have to calculate the time in hours. If it is easier, use weeks. However make sure that the trainer is working on the project for full weeks, ie don't put in the application a course of only 10 hours a week for 12 weeks and then claim 12 full weeks for the trainer without an explanation, eg "this is a 10 hour a week course with three separate groups of beneficiaries being trained each week."

Example II

This is a 12 week course, with one trainer working full time on it for those weeks. He also requires 2 weeks preparation time. He works full time for the organisation with four weeks annual leave and 2 weeks public holiday, so he is at work for 46 weeks (52 – 4 – 2). His salary at present is £14,500 plus employers' NIC of £1,508 and pension of £1,015 making total salary costs of £17,023. However there is a negotiated pay increase of 2% which takes effect next April before the project starts so you need to add that on. This makes next year's salary cost £17,363 (£17,023 plus 2%). The trainer's salary chargeable to ESF is therefore

$$\frac{£17,363}{46 \text{ weeks}} \quad \times \quad 14 \text{ weeks} \quad = \quad £5,284.39$$

b) Non teaching staff may also keep timesheets, but this may prove more difficult. Managers and administration staff work for the organisation as a whole of which the ESF projects are usually only a part. Therefore it may be preferable to treat the non teaching staff as an overhead and use the overhead apportionment figure when calculating their salary costs attributable to the ESF project.

In order to calculate a meaningful overhead apportionment figure, go through the following stages:

- list all the staff who will be working in the organisation within the year, including external trainers for the ESF, (for example 6 staff members at 1,589 hours per person),

- calculate how many hours or, if you prefer, weeks they will be at work during the year (eg 9,534 hours ie 6 x 1,589),

- take out any managers or admin staff who will have a role to play in the ESF project but whose time will be difficult to apportion (eg take out 2,384 hours ie 1.5 staff x 1,589 hours),

- add up the total hours for all the staff employed by the organisation (including the external trainers) but excluding the managers and admin staff as above (eg 7,150 hours in the example ie 9,534 minus 2,384),

- add up the total staff hours for the ESF project (for this example, say 500 hours)

- divide the ESF staff hours by the total staff hours and you have an apportionment figure that you can use for all the eligible overheads as well as for the non teaching staff. The figure will become more manageable if you multiply it by 100 and use as a percentage.

For the example, this is $\dfrac{500}{7,150}$ or multiply by 100 to get 7% rate of apportionment

See Appendix 3 for further examples of apportionment.

2. Apportionment based on beneficiary hours

This is a useful apportionment calculation to use if you are trying to apportion certain costs between ESF training projects, for example, the costs of an outside evaluator. It is even more useful if the business of your organisation is purely training or working directly with students/clients, in which case you can use the beneficiary hours' apportionment for overheads and other shared costs. It is also the best method to use if you have ESF eligible and non ESF eligible beneficiaries on the same training course.

You must take care that you take all factors into account when apportioning on beneficiary hours. You must include the number of beneficiaries and course length in the calculation.

Example

You have 4 ESF projects as follows

A   10 beneficiaries doing 200 hours each
B   18 beneficiaries doing 200 hours each
C   7 beneficiaries doing 546 hours each
D   25 beneficiaries doing 600 hours each

The hours per project are as follows:

A   2,000   (10 x 200)
B   3,600   (18 x 200)
C   3,822   (7 x 546)
D   15,000   (25 x 600)

The total number of hours is 24,422

Thus any shared costs between the projects can be divided by 24,422 and multiplied by the number of hours of each project, or you can calculate the percentage for each project.

A is 2,000/24,422 x 100 = 8%
B is 3,600/24,422 x 100 = 15%
C is 3,822/24,422 x 100 = 16%
D is 15,000/24,422 x 100 = 61%

See Appendix 4 for further examples of apportionment based on beneficiary hours.

3.   Apportionment based on the length of the course

This method only applies when your organisation concentrates all its resources on one ESF course for a particular period, or where the project is operated at its own separate venue having separable costs.

For example an organisation runs a substantial ESF project for 39 weeks of the year. It does no other work during that time. Then overheads could be apportioned using the number of ESF weeks divided by the number of weeks in the year ie $\dfrac{39}{52}$.

4.   Apportionment based on space/area

This method is used for apportioning particular types of overheads. These are rent and leasing of buildings, business rate, water rate, heat and light, cleaning, building maintenance, building insurance. You need to know the square footage of the organisation's building or part of a building. Then measure the square footage of the area the ESF project will be using. If the project is running full time from January to December, it is then correct to divide the ESF square footage by the total square footage and use that apportionment to charge the relevant costs to the ESF project.

However it is more likely that you will not be running full time for a whole year so you will then have to further apportion the costs taking into account the number of weeks and the hours per week that the space will be used for the project.

See Appendix 5 for example of apportionment based on space/area.

5.   Apportionment based on actual recorded usage

You may consider that the ESF project will use some of the organisation's resources at a greater rate than the figures show using some of the other methods of apportionment. For example, beneficiaries may use the telephone a great deal as part of their training or, there may be an inordinate amount of photocopying. In these cases you will **need** to set up systems to record the actual use. With telephone costs you can arrange for itemised billing, or have a dedicated line installed. With some photocopiers you can install a key system which records numbers of copies per person or department.

It may be difficult to budget for these at application stage, but you do need to try and reach a **realistic** figure. For example, there will be 10 beneficiaries doing market research over the telephone for 4 weeks at an average cost of £20 per week per beneficiary – cost £800. Then at final claim stage you can claim the **actual** costs based on the records of actual use.

Checking the income

You must check that you have sufficient eligible income to cover all of the costs. List all the available income, including ESF, public match funding, private match funding, and revenue income. Take care with match funding in-kind – you can only use eligible costs paid by the match funder on behalf of the project and they must be willing to provide documentary evidence to substantiate all of the match funded costs. If the income is of varying types and comes from a variety of sources, prepare an income profile which shows each of the costs against the related income i.e. the source of the income and amount.

Taking the budget seriously

The percentage or fraction of the shared costs charged to the ESF project must be properly worked out so that it looks **reasonable.** The figures in the application form are not cast in stone, you are allowed to vire money between budget headings throughout the ESF period. However there are good reasons why it is important to take time to get realistic figures together for the budget:

-    if you have some strange looking amounts with no detail (eg "General overheads – £30,000") or lots of round amounts in the budget (ie every figure is rounded to the nearest £1,000), then you may not get through the selection process;

- you may be including figures that are below the true cost, so that the project is not viable or the organisation suffers financial difficulties;

- you may be including figures that are substantially more than the true cost, in which case the project may look too expensive to fund, or, if it does gain funding, you will be taking up monies that could be used by other projects.

If you are serious about running ESF funded training courses, then you need to treat the budgeting process seriously too. Consider each of the budget lines separately and keep copious notes as to how you arrived at the figures. You are going to need them!

Section 3 Match funding

What is an ESF public match funder?

All ESF projects require some element of public match funding in place in order for them to be eligible. You can be in receipt of public match funding from more than one source. However one of the match funders must agree to take on a monitoring role – they then become the lead match funder. The following organisations are eligible to provide public match funding:

1. a central government body

2. a local government body

3. a non profit making organisation, whether incorporated or un-incorporated, registered with the Charity Commission. That registration must be maintained throughout the period of the claim for ESF support. In Scotland the charity would require to be recognised by the Inland Revenue

4. any organisation which directly or indirectly receives over 50% of its core funding from central government, local government or levies raised for training purposes. The calculation should be based on the previous financial year's receipts, excluding any EU monies and there must also be over 50% income, excluding any EU monies forecast for the following year.

Any organisation drawing down match funding from another public body (either in cash or in-kind) solely and exclusively to run a specific ESF project will be required to submit a separate Public Match Funding Certificate signed by that public body for the match funding provided.

If your organisation considers that it can act as its own public match funder because it falls into one of the four categories detailed above, then it may have to provide proof of this at a verification visit.

Private match funding

Private match funding is allowed but there must be some public sector match funding for projects – the minimum percentage will be stated in the current guidance notes. Private match funders are defined as any money originating from private enterprise, including:

> public limited companies
>
> private companies
>
> partnerships
>
> co-operatives
>
> self-employed people

The audit trail for match funding

If you have a verification visit from the Verification and Audit Section of the ESF Unit or from the European Commission, they will check that the match funding is eligible. This means that the source of the funding must be eligible, that the funds did contribute toward the eligible costs of the project and that there is verifiable evidence of this.

Funds which include or have already been used to attract EC funding cannot be used as match funding. Some monies from Government programmes can be used as match funding but great care must be taken if you are planning to go down that route. *Work-Based Training for Adults* and *Work Based Training for Young People (National Traineeships and other training strands)* **are not eligible** to use as match funding by non government applicants. In principle other Government programmes can be used to match fund ESF, but check very carefully the current rules as these are complex and do not apply equally across all ESF Objectives.

There must be clear audit trails for both public and private match funding. This may present particular problems where the match funding provided by another organisation is in-kind. You need to have written evidence of the agreement with the match funder and make it clear to them what they will need to provide for audit purposes. The in-kind support must be verifiable by auditors and backed up by source documentation (so, for example if the local authority is providing officer time as in-kind match funding, this must be backed up by payroll records within the local authority). Match funding in-kind cannot include any depreciation costs or purchase of capital equipment.

If your organisation considers that it can act as its own match funder because it falls into one of the four categories detailed above, then it may have to provide proof of this at a verification visit.

Responsibilities of an ESF public match funder

The match funder must

- contribute to the actual eligible costs of the project

- inform the applicant and either the secretariat or the ESF Unit promptly of any changes to the match funding provision or agreement

- take full responsibility for ensuring that they are eligible to be a public match funder and that the funds are eligible to match ESF funds

- carry out regular and formal monitoring of the project to ensure that effective management and financial controls exist in order to comply with EU regulations. At the beginning of the project the match funder is expected to be able to confirm the financial viability of the applicant and agree to inform the secretariat at any point should this seem to be a problem.

What you need your public match funder to do

External public match funders are required to sign to certify that they are aware of and agree to all of the above responsibilities. At the time of writing this is done through the *Public Match Funding Certificate (PMFC),* and each public match funder has to sign one of these for each amount of match funding it is providing for each ESF application. No ESF monies can be approved and paid until all of the PMFCs are properly completed, signed and stamped with the official stamp of the match funder and received by the ESF Unit or relevant secretariat.

With the approval letter you receive from the ESF Unit (or secretariat), there will be a First Advance and a Second Advance Claim Form. You complete the First Advance Claim Form and return it to the ESF Unit (or secretariat) in order to release the first 50% of ESF monies. However, the lead public match funder has also to sign and stamp the form. Similarly, when you have spent half of the first advance, you can claim the second advance payment of 30% of the approved ESF amount; again the lead public match funder has to sign and stamp the form.

After the project has finished, usually after the end of the ESF year, the organisation completes an ESF Final Claim Form which details the actual outcomes of the project including the actual costs. At this stage the amounts of match funding may change. If you have underspent you may reduce the amount of matching monies. If you have over spent you may have accessed further public monies to make up the difference, so have more matching funding. At the final claim stage all the public match funders are obliged to sign a General Statement of Expenditure (GSE), which states that the project ran as detailed in the final claim documentation and that they provided a specific amount of monies towards the project costs. Again the GSE has to be signed and stamped with the official stamp of the organisation providing the match funding.

You need your public match funder to acknowledge their responsibilities as ESF match funders. They may not understand ESF funding and their role within it. You should work with your match funders in order to familiarise them with the ESF rules including the eligibility criteria for beneficiaries, what are eligible costs and the application and claim procedures. Make sure that they are aware of the detail of your project, involving them at the planning stage if appropriate. Give them a copy of your application and final claim forms and ask them for any comments. Keep them informed of any significant changes to the project and consider including them in any evaluation of the training.

You may need to be even more pro-active within the relationship you establish with the project's lead match funder, who has the responsibility of monitoring the project. Invite them to look at your record-keeping systems, both during the life of the project and at the final claim stage. Make sure that they are clear what your objectives and performance criteria are. Give them a copy of the ESF Unit's Verification and Audit Section GUIDE FOR APPLICANTS booklet. Make them aware of their responsibilities and then show them how best they can fulfil those responsibilities.

In-kind match funding

There must be clear audit trails for both public and private match funding.This may present particular problems where the match funding provided by another organisation is in-kind.

Match funding (MF) in-kind is where an *external* organisation or individual provides a service (or product) free of charge to an ESF project.The cost of the service or product can then be used as match funding if all of the following points apply:

- it is covering ESF eligible costs

- the organisation (or individual) providing the service or product agrees to its use as matching funding

- the organisation (or individual) providing the service or product can provide evidence of the costs

- the costs are included in the breakdown of expenditure on the application form

You need to have written evidence of the agreement with the match funder and make it clear to them what they will need to provide for audit purposes.The in-kind support must be verifiable by auditors and backed up by source documentation.

In-kind match funding represents the value of goods and services that the match funder has supplied for the ESF project and that they have agreed can be used as matching money for ESF funding. Some examples of in-kind matching are:

- salaries of staff seconded to work on the project

- photocopier services

- use of telephone line

- with effect from 1998, volunteer time can be used as match funding

Volunteer Time

Projects can now use unpaid volunteer time as **private** match funding in-kind. However projects should be aware that in order for volunteer time to be eligible, it must be covering only volunteers acting in a wholly voluntary capacity. Any paid employee of the organisation who performs additional voluntary duties will not be eligible. Also, remember this is not paid seconded staff from other organisations (which are already eligible under match funding rules).

The method of evaluating volunteer time for match funding purposes is as follows:

1. Determine what project tasks will be undertaken by volunteers

2. Categorise them into the following roles as far as possible:

    *   Project Manager

    *   Project Co-ordinator

    *   Project Researcher

    *   Project Administrator

    *   Trainer

3. Determine how many hours each person in each role will spend on the project in the year.

4. Cost the hours using the official notional hourly rates issued by the ESF Unit (see current guidance notes for details)

5. **These hourly rates *include* all (notional) on-costs such as Employers' NIC and pensions.** Try wherever possible to match the tasks to be performed by your volunteers with the above examples. The reason for this is that it may delay project approval if you include different rates for volunteer time. Where a project has a volunteer performing the same duties as a paid employee on the project, the rate allowed for unpaid volunteer time will be whichever is the lower of the following:

    *   the notional rate, or

    *   the rate paid to the equivalent paid employee.

If you are planning to use volunteer time as match funding you must take steps to keep proper records including detailed time sheets for all volunteers used on the project.

What is not eligible as in-kind support

Match funding in-kind **cannot** include the following:

- any depreciation costs

- purchase of capital equipment

- ESF ineligible costs such as finance costs, consultancy costs

- costs which are ineligible because they were incurred outside the ESF period

- notional costs (i.e. with no clear reason for charging that amount)

- any profit element within the match funding

As with direct match funding, in-kind match funding must not contain any element of European Union monies.

Remember that you can only include ESF eligible costs paid by the match funder for project expenditure incurred during the relevant ESF year.

The match funder providing in-kind matching monies for your project must be willing to sign all the documentation necessary for you to access ESF funding. They must also provide you with written evidence of the agreement and detail of the types of expenditure and amounts involved. See Appendix 6 for an example of this.

When match funding in-kind takes the form of a donation of staff time, then the match funder should provide an invoice detailing the amount of time the person spent on the project, their salary details and the apportioned 'cost' of that member of staff to the project. (In addition time sheets should also be available to support the amount of time they have spent on the project.) This applies whether the in-kind match funding comes from a public or private source.

Accounting for match funding

You must be able to identify the ESF match funding in your organisation's financial records. Remember that the ESF monies are not eligible if you did not have the match funding in place.

Section 4 Managing ESF finance throughout the year

1. Good financial systems need to be in place before you start

The records necessary for ESF funded projects are extremely detailed and must relate to your organisation's main financial records.Therefore you must have good systems in place before you design and implement the extra record keeping needed for ESF. It may be helpful to list some of the possible problems that need to be tackled within different sizes of organisations.

a) Small organisations

- Often small organisations have limited financial skills within the existing staff. It is vital that some staff understand basic accounting and the extra records necessary for ESF. Documentation must be filed in order so that it is easily retrievable for final claim preparation and possible audit visits.

- Related to this is the fact that some organisations use a volunteer, who may or may not be well qualified, to do the finance work. In this case make sure that the work is kept up to date at all times.

- Even when the skills are available in house, small voluntary organisations often see the administration work as being secondary to their main work, which is the reason they are there. This view is understandable, but erroneous if ESF projects are to be run.The importance of the administrative function must be given proper recognition.

- Small organisations often use a very simple system for recording finances consisting of an analysed cash book and petty cash book.

This may not be adequate for ESF purposes, especially if they are planning to run more than one project.

- In order to get the most from limited resources, small organisations often negotiate a very low price on their annual audit. However in most cases you get the level of service that you pay for, and an auditor who has had his/her fee negotiated down to, say, £400 for a company audit, probably doesn't have enough time to familiarise her/himself with the ESF regulations. Company auditors carry out their work according to the requirements of the relevant law, e.g. Companies Act 1985. They will not audit your ESF project unless you ask them to and they will need full details of the ESF regulations.

b) Larger organisations

- The problems with larger organisations seem to be mostly based on communication difficulties. For example the person who is recruiting the trainees does not know that the project is funded by ESF and therefore there are certain eligibility criteria that must be met e.g. for priority 3.2 beneficiaries have to be aged 16 to 24 years, and so they recruit ineligible beneficiaries.

- Similarly, it may be that no-one informed the finance staff (or indeed consulted them) that extra records needed to be kept for ESF purposes and so none were kept.

- Organisations (and this applies to both large and small ones) who have been accessing ESF for a number of years (and have not been audited recently) become blasé about ESF and the need to keep good, up to date records.

- In very large organisations financial systems can be very complex and difficult to adapt.

2. Adapting your records for ESF

a) Direct costs

Direct costs (for example external trainers, beneficiary travel) can be included as a total in your main financial records. If you have a simple system consisting of an analysed cash book, then one of the columns can be used for the ESF project expenditure. If you have a double entry system using ledgers, you can open a ledger account for ESF direct costs. Your auditor can then use this figure when s/he prepares your annual accounts. On its own though, this total for direct costs is not enough for monitoring expenditure and for final claim information. You will need to further analyse this figure into the expenditure headings you have already specified in your ESF project application. This should be done monthly and the total must balance to the total ESF direct costs in your main books of account. You can use a computer spreadsheet, analysis paper or an analysis book. You should include full details of each expense, including date, document reference number, detail of the expense and the amount.

See Appendix 7 for an example.

b) Apportioned costs over ESF projects only
The above example relates to individual ESF projects. If you are running two or more projects you may incur some expenditure that is shared by all of the projects (eg consumables, costs of an outside evaluation). You can treat this by either:

i) splitting each invoice total for shared costs accordingly as they are received, charging the relevant percentage to each project,

or

ii) by putting all of these invoices to a ledger account or cash book column for "ESF project costs – shared". Apportionment and further analysis will then be required for monitoring expenditure (monitoring points are usually in June and October each year) and final claim purposes.

c) Apportioned salary costs
You need to have a mechanism in place for analysing the salary costs to ESF. How you do this depends on the system you have in place for reconciling salaries.

Basically, the salary costs to an organisation consist of the gross salaries of employees, employers' National Insurance Contributions (NIC) and (if paid) employer's pension contribution (sometimes called superannuation). However these amounts are not actually paid out of the bank as separate sums all in the same period. They are paid as follows:

- net salaries (ie gross salaries less PAYE and employees' NIC and employees' pension deductions, and sometimes other deductions, such as trade union subscriptions) are paid in the month they are due, either by cheque to individuals or, more commonly by BACS which comes out of the bank as a lump sum,

- payments to the Inland Revenue of PAYE, employees' NIC and employers' NIC are usually paid the month *after* the month in which the salary payment is made, usually by cheque (sometimes payments are made every three months),

- payments to pension providers of both the employees' and the employers' pension contributions, sometimes paid in the same month as the salary payment, sometimes later, usually paid by direct debit.

- payments to the relevant body of the other deductions made from salaries, eg to the trade union for union subs, to the court for attachments of earnings. These may be paid by cheque, BACS or direct debit.

All of these payments need to be reconciled and the actual costs (gross salaries, employers' NIC and employers' pension payments) apportioned for ESF purposes.

Large organisations will have systems in place for reconciling salary costs. For small organisations, they should keep a payroll book and each month should reconcile the salaries as follows:

Gross salaries		Net Salaries paid to employees
+		+
Employers' NIC	*should equal*	Amount to be paid to Inland Revenue
+		+
Employer's pension costs		Amount paid to pension provider
		+
		Amounts to be paid for other deductions from salaries

Once you have the salary cost each month you can further analyse these between ESF projects and non ESF activity.

See Appendix 8 for an example of this.

d) Apportioning overhead costs

The overhead costs you are apportioning must be linked with the costs in your main financial records. This will mean that you are going to have to prepare management accounts on a regular basis so that you can monitor your ESF spend. The reason for this is that overhead expenses in general are not incurred regularly each month over the year. For example, you may pay rent three months in advance and insurance one year in advance, business rates and telephone costs can be in advance and in arrears, photocopying charges may be in arrears. So when management accounts are prepared you will have to accrue for some costs and reduce others (these are prepayments).

When the accounts are prepared, you can then apply the percentages or fractions in order to apportion between ESF projects and non ESF activity.

3. Working papers

Working papers are the pieces of paper you use to back up the figures you are claiming for ESF. They need to be clear, neat and easy to read, be able to be easily checked and be easily retrievable. Bodies auditing ESF will want to see all of the working papers that relate to the project they are checking.

Examples of working papers are:

- the calculations used in constructing the budget as shown on the ESF application form

- the research done to find information that you have used in the application form – these are the costings, the numbers of beneficiaries to be recruited, hours to be spent in training, likely numbers of beneficiaries into jobs etc, likely qualifications gained by beneficiaries

- detail of how the apportionment calculations were made

- schedules or spreadsheet used to break down the information contained in the organisation's main accounts to show the actual costs of the ESF project

- the written method used to regularly check that the costs of the project are in line with the budget

- the calculations used to construct the final claim form detail

- the breakdown of staff salary costs into separate ESF projects and non ESF activity

- the analysis of the actual trainee hours as shown on the final claim form.

The working papers must be clearly referenced to the ESF project to which they refer. (Up to and including 1997, each ESF project has a unique *dossier number and letter* e.g. 972356UK3C; from 1998 each project will have a unique *dossier number*). It is also important that papers are filed in an obvious place so that any new staff to the organisation are able to access and understand the information in subsequent years.

4. Proofs of payment and the audit trail

The audit trail is extremely important for your ESF administration. The DfEE's booklet "Audit of European Social Fund Projects" states *"It is clearly important, therefore to ensure that all claims are backed up by detailed working papers with a visible audit trail between the final claim, the annual returns and the supporting source documentation"*.

It is little use having a file or an accounting book labelled "ESF Finance" containing details of all the expenditure incurred by your ESF project if this information does not relate to your organisation's main accounting records, the annual accounts, invoices and salary records.

The expenditure totals on schedules or spreadsheet you are using to analyse ESF costs must relate to costs shown in the main financial records. They must also be easily referenced to source documentation.

So, for example, the rent costs will have been taken from the management accounts for the period. The actual figure is the one on the trial balance which is made up of invoices for rent and possibly a journal entry to adjust for the rent paid in advance.

ESF auditors will want to examine documentation relating to the costs shown in the final claim. Thus you need to have paperwork to prove all your expenditure. Examples of these are:

Suppliers invoices - these should be proper invoices with the name and address of the supplier, the date, details of the goods or services supplied. This includes payments to registered child minders. Invoices should be originals; photocopies of invoices are not usually acceptable for audit purposes.

Petty cash vouchers - for small amounts only and with a receipt attached where possible.

Pro forma for
beneficiary expenses - these are very important if you are paying beneficiaries money direct eg as an allowance or travel; auditors always check that you are paying beneficiaries properly and you must get original signatures whenever you pay allowances or expenses. The forms should show dates, details and amounts as well as signatures. Receipts should be attached where possible. You should get beneficiaries to sign for payment even when you are paying them by cheque or by BACS.

Pro forma for
staff travel
and subsistence - these should show dates, detail of the journey, method of travel and mileage where appropriate as well as signatures of claimants. Receipts for train tickets, taxis and subsistence should be attached.

Salary books/records - these are kept to back up the salary costs claimed.

Bank statements - auditors may wish to check that certain payments, particularly large ones have been paid and gone through the bank account. They may also wish to check that match funding has been received.

Written evidence of
any in-kind matching - This would need to come from your match funder on their letterhead and be signed. It should be an original document and detail all of the goods and services including actual amounts provided in-kind. When match funding in kind takes the form of a donation

of staff time, the applicant should hold a notional invoice for the 'cost' of that member of staff to their project. This invoice should be provided, regardless of whether the match funding in kind is from the public or private sector. *Remember you must be sure that there is an audit trail leading to original documentation to back up the actual costs incurred by the organisation providing the in-kind match funding.*

Copies of the organisation's audited accounts — this is the latest set of audited accounts. The ESF project income and costs should be detailed somewhere, possibly in a note to the accounts.

It is important to remember that the ESF period runs from January to December each year. (The Community Initiatives can be over longer periods but have to be accounted for by calendar year). In order for your expenditure to be eligible, it must have been incurred within the January to December period, i.e. the activity has to have taken place within the relevant ESF period. So check at the end of the training period that you have received all the invoices you were expecting. If, for example, one of your external trainers is late invoicing you and dates the invoice January 1999 for ESF training done in November and December 1998, make sure she details the dates of the training on the invoice.

5. Rules on payment of advances

With the approval letter you receive, there is a First Advance Claim Form and a Second Advance Claim Form. When you are ready to start the project you can claim the first advance payment which is 50% of the approved ESF amount by completing this form and sending it to the relevant secretariat. When you have spent half of the first advance, i.e. you have spent 25% of the ESF approved amount, you can claim the second advance payment. You complete the Second Advance Claim Form and send it to the secretariat. The second advance is 30% of the ESF approved amount.

The rule on claiming second advance payments is very strict and, at an audit visit, you will be expected to show how you knew you had spent half of the first advance when you claimed the second advance.

So you need to be preparing reports on your actual ESF spend on a regular basis.

6.   ESF Monitoring forms

You will be required to complete a monitoring form at least once within the ESF year and probably twice, usually in June and October. The form is very simple and asks you to state whether the project is progressing as outlined in the application form and whether you can identify any underspends. Remember to declare only the amount of ESF underspend.

If the project is running as stated and there are no underspends, then you tick the relevant boxes and send off the forms as instructed. If the project is not running to plan you are asked for amended figures. If you have identified underspend then you should put in the amount and send off as instructed.

However, take care – once you have officially notified ESF underspend, that amount is then deducted from the amount that was originally approved for your project and you cannot subsequently change your mind and decide you made a mistake or you now need the money.

That is not to say that you should never identify underspends on the monitoring forms. Underspends are used to fund other projects within your region and you need to identify them at as early a stage as possible. You need to take care that you are certain that they are truly not required by the project. You do this by checking the actual figures against the budget figures and look for differences. These are called variances. Analyse the variances by looking back at your budget notes to see what assumptions you made at the time you put the application together.

For example you may have assumed that you would be paying for childcare for 25 children but in the event there are only 10 children for whom you are paying childcare. If all the other costs are more or less on target then you will not need all of the ESF in your application, so you can identify underspends.

If you under spent and did not notify the relevant secretariat you may be penalised in the selection process in subsequent years.

7.   Significant changes to your project

If there are significant changes to the project, then you need to inform the relevant secretariat and get confirmation in writing that it is OK. Significant changes are defined in ESF guidance notes. The ones that relate to financial information are as follows:

- variance of the overall unit cost of more than 20% (the unit cost is the total project costs divided by the total number of beneficiary hours)

- virement (movement of money) of more than 20% between expenditure headings (i.e. staff costs, beneficiary costs, other costs) within a project without additional items being claimed

- virement of money between projects within an application (if permitted)

- additional items of expenditure being claimed during the life of the application

- changes in matching funding

Items of expenditure not approved during the period of the application will not be accepted at final claim stage. You are obliged to inform the relevant secretariat of any significant changes to the project. You cannot include significant changes to the project at final claim stage unless you have had written agreement from the secretariat.

If there are significant changes to the project and the secretariat has **not** been informed, you may be required to repay some or all of the ESF monies received to date.

Section 5 Problems – issues to address

European Social Fund money is not easy money. Administration must be tight in order to comply with the regulations. Someone within your organisation has to have some fairly specific financial skills, including budgeting, cash flow forecasting, analysis of costs, preparation of management accounts. You can't make a profit from ESF. There can be severe payment delays.

Some common problems or difficulties not covered so far are:

- the cash flows

- revenue income

- loss of revenue because ESF is using resources within the organisation that are normally charged for at a profit

- depreciation

- value added tax (VAT)

- leasing of equipment

1. The cash flows

It is probably necessary at this stage to highlight the difference between an *ESF project* and an *ESF application.* So far, we have concentrated on stressing the need for separate budgets and financial records for each project. However for the years up to and including 1997, when you applied for ESF funding you were able to group a certain number of projects into one application. The projects within one application must be for the same objective, priority and (if applicable) measure. Details of *project* activity including expenditure, beneficiaries trained, outturns must be recorded separately. However approval letters are issued and the advances and final claims are paid *by application,* not by project.

ESF monies are paid in three stages.The first advance is for 50% of the approved allocation and can be claimed immediately following approval, or as the project has started, if later (for 1997, if there is more than one project in an application it is when the first project starts, if later).The second advance is for 30% of the ESF allocation approved and can be claimed when you have spent **half** of the first advance.The balance of ESF, which may be 20% or less is paid in arrears, usually 11 to 12 months *after* the end of the ESF year.

This may not seem too bad, especially if you are planning a fairly small project.The problem is that you cannot be paid ESF monies until all the paperwork has been correctly completed, received, checked and processed by the relevant secretariat. Past experience has shown that payments are usually delayed for a variety of reasons so you need to be planning accordingly.

The first thing to do is to prepare a cash flow forecast for the organisation in order to highlight where there may be some difficulties and also to look at ways of dealing with the potential problems associated with cash flow.

One way of making the cash flow healthier is to negotiate with your match funder that they pay you all of the match funding up front or at least load the payments at the start of the project.

Another possible mechanism for dealing with this problem is to identify some of your costs, for which you can delay payment. For example, you may be able to order supplies of stationery and other materials through a central purchasing function of your local authority, who will agree to await payment until you receive ESF funds. If you contract out some of your training to a college, then write into the contract (if you can) that they will receive payment as soon as your ESF funds are received.

You may be able to negotiate an interest free loan from your match funder.

You may be obliged to negotiate a loan or overdraft facility with your bank. However there are costs associated with this which you cannot then reclaim from ESF.

2. Revenue income

Revenue income is income generated by the ESF project, and the rule is that it must be used to offset the costs of the project i.e. you cannot generate income from your ESF project and then keep that money to use for some other activity within your organisation.

Examples of revenue income are:

- sale of training produce (e.g. meals, plants, furniture)

- sale of services (e.g. gardening, childcare, home help services)

- use of training facilities for other fee earning courses or for hire

- course fees charged to individuals

- receipts from various sources (e.g. canteen, phones, postage, photocopying, insurance claims, crèche charges).

If your organisation is part funded by ESF and the organisation itself earns income from, for example the canteen, then part of that income belongs to the ESF project(s) and must be apportioned accordingly. If your organisation is charging part of its overhead costs to ESF and it earns revenue income that relates to those overheads, then the net amount of the overhead should be used when calculating the amount to be charged to ESF.

For example,

Your annual rent is £8,500. You rent out rooms to groups and the rental income from this is £1,900. The ESF overhead apportionment percentage is 33.33%

You must net off the £1,900 from the £8,500 and use the net cost of rent of £6,600 as the overhead figure for ESF purposes. The ESF charge would therefore be £6,600 at 33.33% ie £2,200.

Revenue income can't be used to match fund ESF.

If you are unsure if income should be used to offset ESF project costs always ask for advice at the outset – don't wait to see if you can get away with it as you may be liable to repay monies at a later date.

Example:

Your ESF project's total costs are £58,000

You estimate that from sale of training produce you will earn £3,000

The ESF, match funding and revenue are made up as follows,

Revenue	£3,000
ESF	£24,750 This is 45% of £55,000 (£58,000 less £3,000)
Public match funding	£30,250 This is 55% of £55,000
Total costs	£58,000

You can then adjust the figures at final claim stage, remembering that you can't claim more than the ESF approved amount.

In the example the total costs at final claim stage were £59,312. The revenue income was much higher than estimated at £5,117.

The ESF, match funding and revenue at final claim are made up as follows:

Revenue	£5,117
ESF	£24,387 This is 45% of £54,195 (£59,312 less £5,117)
Public match funding	£29,808 This is 55% of £54,195
Total costs	£59,312

3. Loss of revenue

Some ESF project promoters have tried to invoice at a commercial rate for services they provide in house for the ESF project. This is not allowed.

For example, an organisation specialises in information technology training charged to companies at a commercial rate. They also hire out their suites of computer equipment to other organisations at a commercial rate. If the organisation then becomes an ESF applicant, they will be obliged to use their equipment to train ESF beneficiaries *at cost*. They cannot charge the use of the suite of computers to the ESF project at their normal rates. The actual costs associated with the computers such as depreciation of the equipment, maintenance and cleaning can be considered as eligible items of expenditure.

Revenue associated with lost opportunity is notional and therefore ineligible.

4. Depreciation

If you wish to claim depreciation costs these should relate to your organisation's depreciation policy. If the depreciation policy used for calculating depreciation costs for your ESF project *differs* from the depreciation policy of your organisation, there has to be a very good reason for this. You would have to fully justify this if you were audited.

You can use different methods of depreciation. However the *minimum* number of years you can depreciate over is normally 3 years.

This means that for straight line depreciation, you can claim a maximum of one third of the costs of purchasing your fixed assets. For reducing balance method of depreciation the maximum percentage you can claim is 66.67% of the current written down value.

If your organisation is in receipt of capital grants towards the cost of fixed assets, then the grants should be deducted from the costs of the fixed asset before depreciation costs are calculated for ESF purposes. Where your organisation uses deferred credits to offset depreciation costs, the amount of the deferred credit must be deducted from the depreciation costs for ESF purposes.

Example:

A photocopier is purchased at a cost of £20,000 but the organisation received a grant of £7,500 towards the cost. The photocopier's life is 5 years and depreciation will be on a straight line basis . There is no residual value. **Thus the annual depreciation is £20,000/5 i.e. £4,000**

However, the £7,500 will be treated as a reserve (i.e. the full amount will not be included as income in the year it was received) and each year one fifth of it will be brought into income in order to offset the depreciation costs. **Thus there will be income each year (called a deferred credit) of £7,500/5 i.e. £1,500**

Provided that the fixed assets are being used for ESF purposes, the organisation is able to claim depreciation (apportioned where necessary) as follows:

Depreciation	£4,000
LESS Deferred credit	(£1,500)
Total depreciation to apportion to ESF	£2,500

The depreciation charged must relate to the ESF year and may then need to be apportioned to reflect the usage of the equipment for the ESF project. If you intend to base depreciation costs on usage of equipment, the usage has to be supported by documentation.

You may have difficulties if you have a different financial year to the ESF year.

Example:

Your organisation's financial year ends on 31st March 1999, what do you put in as depreciation in the final claim for the ESF period ending 31st December 1998, assuming that the ESF project has been running all year?

First of all look at your annual accounts for the year ending 31st March 1998, then calculate 25% of the depreciation figure in those accounts in respect of owned equipment being used for ESF purposes, as this represents the period January to March 1998.

Then you need to calculate the depreciation figure for the period April 1998 to March 1999. Try to follow the method used in the previous year's accounts. Add any fixed assets bought during the period, leave out any assets that have been fully depreciated already, deduct any assets that have been disposed of. Then deduct any capital grants received towards the assets. When you have calculated the depreciation amount, take 75% of it to represent the period April to December 1998.

Add the figures for the two periods together and you have the depreciation costs for the ESF year. You will probably then have to apportion this figure between different ESF projects and non ESF activity. **Make sure that you keep a copy of the workings!**

See Appendix 9 for an example.

5. Value Added Tax (VAT)

You must be absolutely clear about the status of VAT and ESF within your organisation *before* you apply for ESF funding. There are two possibilities regarding ESF and VAT;

- it may be that HM Customs & Excise rule that ESF is outside the scope of VAT, in which case you can not reclaim the VAT on your ESF expenditure from HM Customs & Excise. However, you can claim VAT costs from ESF. So if you bought an item of equipment for your project for £100 plus 17.5% VAT, you would claim £117.50 from ESF.

- it may be that HM Customs & Excise rule that you can reclaim the VAT on your ESF project costs, in which case you would claim the net cost of items of expenditure from the ESF. So if you bought an item of equipment for your project for £100 plus 17.5% VAT, you would claim £100.00 from ESF and £17.50 from HM Customs and Excise.

The ESF Unit are having discussions at present with HM Customs & Excise and there does not seem to be a definitive answer on whether ESF projects are outside the scope of VAT or not. The matter of VAT and ESF is a difficult issue and you must take steps to establish and confirm the VAT status of your ESF project at an early stage. You must get confirmation **in writing** from your local VAT office.

If you have any problems on whether to include VAT, contact the relevant secretariat for advice. If you are unsure of your VAT status at ESF application stage, budget the costs to include VAT and note the application form accordingly.

Accounting for VAT on shared ESF costs

If your organisation is registered for VAT but HM Customs & Excise rules that ESF funding is outside the scope of VAT, then you have to split the VAT on shared costs in order to determine how much of the VAT you claim from HM Customs & Excise and how much you claim from ESF.

If you have a simple accounting system, with few invoices being processed then it is easier to split the VAT between ESF (not reclaimable) and non ESF ie trading (reclaimable), at the point where the documentation is entered into the books of account.

Where larger numbers of invoices are processed, it may be preferable to enter all invoices into the system net of VAT and adjust the figures on a monthly or quarterly basis to take account of the proportion of VAT that is outside the scope and cannot be reclaimed. You will need to calculate a proportion of the input tax (VAT on expenditure) that is not reclaimable. You will need to read *Notice 706* available from your local VAT office.

At the end of each month or three months you calculate the amount of input tax you are not able to claim and do a transfer of that amount from the VAT account to the ESF project account. What you are doing is to **charge** to ESF that amount of VAT that you are unable to reclaim because ESF is outside the scope of VAT. You can then show the amount of VAT on shared costs as a separate item on applications and final claim forms.

6.   Leasing of equipment

Auditors will always look at lease agreements as they take different forms. There are two types of commonly used leasing agreements. These are finance leases and operating leases.

A finance lease is similar to a hire purchase agreement in that it is a way of financing the purchase of an asset. The lessee is responsible for all costs of the equipment, including insurance and repairs, and at the end of the lease the asset becomes the property of the lessee. The lease payments on a finance lease are **not** an eligible cost for an ESF project. The leased item should be treated as a fixed asset and depreciated in accordance with the policy of the organisation.

An operating lease is where the ownership of the asset stays with the lessor i.e. it is never going to become the property of the lessee. The lease payments on an operating lease are eligible items of expenditure for an ESF project provided that the costs of the lease are competitive and compare with rates charged in the open market.

Take care with leases, just calling a lease an operating lease in order to make the expenditure ESF eligible will not work – there is an accounting definition of what is a finance lease and all leases are assumed to be finance leases unless proved otherwise.

Section 6 Preparation for final claims

This is a very different task from that at the application stage. At application stage you are doing your best to put an attractive project idea together, trying to make an impression on the selectors and taking care to include as much detail as possible in order to increase your chances of being funded. At final claim stage, you have had most of the money and you know that the balance is going to be a long time coming. You are concentrating your efforts on the present and future work of your organisation and don't wish to be concerned with the past.

The fact is that the great majority of ESF final claims are completed incorrectly. It is difficult to know why this is the case. It is true that deadlines are usually tight which can make things difficult, but the information should have been collected throughout the year and the final claim stage ought to be a matter of bringing the information together and setting it out on the forms.

Stages of preparation for the final claim:

i)   In January bring the cash books up to date, make sure you have your last bank statement for the previous year and do the bank reconciliation.

ii)   Check that you have all outstanding invoices for the previous year. Chase up the ones that are outstanding for ESF projects.

iii)   Enter all invoices for the previous period onto your system.

iv)   Make sure that salary schedules are up to date

v)   Prepare a trial balance.

vi)   Adjust the trial balance figures for accruals and prepayments and prepare the first draft of management accounts up to the end of December. You will have to leave out the ESF project income at this stage as you don't know how much it will be until the final claim forms information has been completed. The period of the management accounts should be from the beginning of your organisation's new financial year to the end of December. So, for example, if your organisation's financial year runs from 1st September to 31st August each year, you will prepare management accounts for the period 1st September to 31st December. If your financial year runs from January to December you will be preparing management accounts that will form the basis of the annual accounts.

vii)   Look at the direct ESF project costs, make sure that they are analysed between the relevant expenditure headings for transfer to the final claim form. Make sure that the total is the same as the total in the main accounts. Check that you haven't inadvertently claimed VAT on any of the costs if your ESF has been ruled as being outside the scope of VAT.

viii)   On the shared costs, check that the rates of apportionment are still valid and if not, adjust them.

ix)   Use the previous period's annual accounts as follows:

Either

a)   apportion the indirect costs (ie shared costs) in the annual accounts in order to ascertain the costs for the period from 1st January to the end of the last financial year. So if the financial year runs from 1st April to 31st March, then your last set of audited accounts will have been up to the end of last March. If you take one quarter of the costs shown in those accounts, it should cover the period January to March,

or

b)   if you ran ESF projects in the previous year, deduct the figures you put together for the end of December management accounts for the last final claim from the figures in the annual accounts. Using the example of an April to March financial year, this will provide the figures for the period January to March,

or

c) you may have a system where you account for shared costs on a monthly basis and can extract the necessary information from this; still you should check that the figures look reasonable against the ones in the annual accounts.

x) The shared costs which you will apportion are the figures from your last set of audited accounts adjusted accordingly,

plus

the figures from the management accounts up to the end of December (unless you have the January to December financial year).

xi) Apportion the shared costs accordingly between separate ESF projects and non ESF activity. You can do this using a computer spreadsheet, analysis paper or an analysis book. Take care if you are using a spreadsheet, as rounding occurs with the result that totals are not always correct.

xii) Make sure salaries are apportioned between ESF projects and non ESF activity.

xiii) Check that you have details of any revenue income that relates to the project.

xiv) Check that you can identify your match funding in your books of account, or if you are using in-kind matching, check that you have the written detail of this from the match funder.

xv) Bring all the working papers together making sure they are referenced to the relevant source documentation and the project dossier number and letter.

xvi) Enter the information onto the final claim forms. It is preferable to do a rough draft first.

An ESF audit/verification visit will be based on the information contained in your final claim forms. If the figures look odd in some way (eg you have put in the exact amounts at final claim that you put in at application), then it is likely that your project will be audited.

All information in the final claim must have the capacity to be proved in some way and ESF records must link to main accounting records and to audited financial statements where possible.

There is an obligation to retain the project records for 3 years *after the receipt of the final payment.*

Section 7 Auditors and audits

There are two groups of auditors having an interest in your ESF records. One group is your company auditors who may need to be educated in the detail of ESF. The other group is those who are responsible for checking that ESF funded training has been properly carried out and full general and financial records kept.

What your company auditors should know about ESF

It is vital that your company auditors understand the effects of European Social Fund monies on your annual accounts. The money is received for the purposes outlined in the ESF application form only. It must not be used for other purposes and the ESF project income and ESF project expenditure must always match. If your auditor does not audit your ESF project expenditure s/he may be overstating income in your annual accounts with potentially devastating results.

The auditor should be able to identify the relevant match funding, at the same time checking that there is no double funding, ie that the same match funding is not being used for more than one ESF project. S/he should check that revenue income is being properly treated and that the organisation is not claiming any ineligible expenditure.

The auditor needs to be aware that any audit visits by the DfEE, the European Commission or the European Court of Auditors will require that the annual accounts are produced and that the information contained in them should relate to information in the final claim forms.

ESF project income should **not** be included in annual accounts as it is *received* but as it is *due*.

Example

- The financial year ends on the 30th September.

- The ESF project runs from January to October at a projected cost of £80,000; ESF funding approved is £36,000 (£80,000 at 45%). The local authority (LA) is providing matching funds of £44,000.

- At the end of September the total costs of the ESF project to date are £72,000. All of the LA money has been received (£44,000) as well as half of the ESF money (£18,000).

Only income which matches the eligible costs for the 9 months January to September should be included in the profit and loss / income and expenditure account. So include

£72,000 at 45%   ESF ie **£32,400**

£72,000 at 55%   LA   ie **£39,600**

£72,000

The differences between the income actually received and that shown in the profit and loss account will appear in the balance sheet.

For the ESF **accrued income** of £32,400 (spent) minus £18,000 (received) ie **£14,400**

For the LA money, **grants received for a specific purpose** of £44,000 (received) minus £39,600 (spent) ie **£4,400.**

The notes to the accounts can include the following "Monies received in respect of ESF projects, are matched against the costs incurred, any balance being carried forward until the project is completed."

Surviving an ESF verification visit

The Verification and Audit Section of the ESF Unit at the DfEE produce a guide detailing what you should expect from an audit visit. They refer to it as a verification visit. The guide is sent to all successful ESF applicants. The guide states "The primary objective of the section is to provide an assurance as to the integrity and reliability of the financial and managerial control systems in place within ESF recipient organisations. It is with this in mind that on-the-spot verification visits are undertaken."

The guide also states the objectives of the visit. The objectives that relate to financial detail are as follows:

"to ensure that the delivery of the project is consistent with the details specified in the approved application and claim form i.e. in line with EC regulations"

"to judge the physical reality of the operations corresponding to the expenditure declared"

"to ensure that the expenditure charged against the project is:

- *real: has the expenditure claimed actually been incurred? Have the percentages for the ESF financial contribution been properly applied?*

- *consistent: was the project in line with the Single Programme Document and was expenditure claimed for relevant to the project?*

- *eligible: does it match the items listed in the eligible costs and was it incurred against activity delivered during the period approved?*

"to ensure that all receipts which may have arisen from the activity are also taken into account, for example: where projects generate their own revenue, this should be declared."

The audit (or verification) visit may be done by the Verification and Audit Section (VAS), by the European Commission (EC) or by the European Court of Auditors (ECA).

Other bodies that are likely to monitor your project are the Government Office in the region or other relevant secretariat. Being monitored by one of these bodies does not preclude you from a verification visit by the VAS or the EC.

A typical verification visit will include the following:

- you will be expected to give a short presentation on the organisation including its structure and objectives, the importance of ESF to the organisation, in particular the percentage of income it affords in relation to other sources of funding, levels of success and future plans,

- testing of the documentation used to put together the final claim financial information, including, for example, invoices, allowance forms signed by beneficiaries, trainer time sheets, financial records, working papers on how costs have been apportioned and how the claim was compiled, match funding documentation, bank statements and copies of audited accounts,

- testing of beneficiary records, including eligibility of beneficiaries, start and finish dates of training, total hours of actual attendance, individual course modules and timetables, beneficiary progress, certificates or qualifications gained, the outcomes of the training.

You will be given between 2 and 4 weeks notice of a visit by the VAS, EC or ECA. The visit will be arranged by telephone and followed up with a formal letter. It is vital that you prepare for the visit and give it a high priority. Key staff must be available to see the verification team if required. These are:

- the person who compiled the application and/or final claim

- the manager of the project

- the person in charge of the finance for the project.

All of the relevant records must be readily available and staff must be on hand to answer questions. If you have found any errors or records are incomplete, it is necessary to inform the verification team at the start of the visit, rather than hoping that they won't discover any mistakes.

You will receive verbal comments on the records at the end of the visit and a written report will be sent to you later. If the team identifies any problems they will outline these in detail at the same time offering solutions. You will then be expected to respond in writing to each point made.

In certain circumstances you may be requested to repay some or all of the ESF monies received for your project(s).

Section 8 Conclusion

There is a need to keep up-to-date good financial records at all times if you wish to run ESF funded projects. There must be someone within your organisation who has good financial skills. The ESF application budget must be properly prepared and notes kept as to how the figures were arrived at. ESF expenditure should be monitored on a regular basis throughout the training period in order to identify underspends at an early stage, check that the project is not over spending, and ascertain that half of the first advance has been spent before the second advance is claimed.

Preparation of final claim information and documentation must be given high priority within the organisation. There must be a clear audit trail to the main financial records, back up documentation must be easily retrievable and working papers numbered with the relevant dossier number and project letter and filed. The company auditor should be fully informed of the rigours of ESF and be asked to audit the final claim documentation.

Other records

There are other (non financial) records that are equally important. These records must show that the project adhered to ESF requirements, to the original application (i.e. you did what you said you were going to do), and to the stipulations of monitoring. All records must have the capacity to be cross referenced.

There should be course records, beneficiary records and staff records. Examples of these are as follows:

Course records will include a course specification, the course programme achieved, a course evaluation.

Beneficiary records will include the following:

- a completed application form signed by the beneficiary with name and address, start and end dates of training, age, length of unemployment (or details of employer if employed in a small or medium size enterprise), qualifications held at the beginning of the course; the form should be checked for eligibility and counter-signed by project management

- analysis of beneficiaries showing age, gender, whether or not they have a disability, ethnicity and status of unemployment

- individual attendance records of beneficiaries showing hourly attendance, type of training (i.e. theory, practical, work experience, guidance and counselling), trainer, venue and module taught

- training modules covered and details of work placements

- qualifications obtained and beneficiaries' destinations; the latter must be followed up after the course ends.

Staff records will consist of staff time sheets showing activity (e.g. training, preparation individual counselling), venue and module taught.

It must then be possible to link the records. So, for example, if one takes the detail of one beneficiary, there should be all the relevant records for that beneficiary and it must be possible to link those records with the staff records and the costs associated with the training, i.e. the salary or invoice, beneficiary allowances, the venue, training materials etc.

The relevant ESF secretariat may be able to recommend (and probably provide) record keeping systems to enable you to satisfy the above requirements.

Other European funds

There is financial support to be had from the EC under other Programmes. In many ways these non Structural Funds are less strict as far as content is concerned. However, after you have applied and been given the go-ahead, you sign a contract and are expected to run the project as stated in the application. (If you don't they may decide not to release interim or final payments). Budgets tend to be a bit more flexible and co-financing (match funding) can come from any source apart from other European funds. Again budgets have to be based on actual costs, you are not allowed to make a profit from the project. The EC contribution is usually less (and can be considerably less) than 50% of total eligible costs.

Most projects are obliged to have at least two partners from different member states. Budgets and final reports are prepared in ECU and you will incur costs in other member states' currencies, so there can be problems with exchange rate fluctuations.

In general, payments come in two or three stages, the final payment being due on receipt of a written report and statement of actual costs.

Be serious about administration

If you are serious about applying for EC funding (including ESF) and running EC funded projects, then you need to be serious about administration. Administration can be a heavy burden on small organisations and it is often seen as a waste of resources. Administrative and finance staff need to be fully informed about the requirements of European funding and consulted on the systems to be set up and run. There are training courses available. Consult your Regional Government Office or keep an eye on the DfEE's newsletter ESF News for details. Remember you can claim the costs of admin staff and their training in your ESF project budget.

If you consider that administration is a drain on time and resources and can't bring yourself to change that, then that's fine, but you cannot in all seriousness think of applying for European funds. However, if you are willing to accept that administration is an integral part of a training project and to put in the time and resources necessary to ensure that records are fully maintained, then you can consider applying for ESF\EU support

APPENDIX 1

Eligible expenditure

ESF eligible expenditure may differ between different funds and from one ESF year to another. Check recent relevant guidelines before you prepare your project budget.

ESF eligible expenditure is detailed in the guidance notes for Objective 3 ESF issued by the Employment Department as follows. It is divided into three categories:

Staff costs

Beneficiary costs

Other costs.

1. Staff costs - the following costs are eligible:

Salaries and wages of staff employed by your organisation plus employer's National Insurance Contributions and pension costs. Staff can include trainers, counsellors, managers, admin staff.

Costs of external trainers can also be claimed.

Travel and subsistence costs for staff can also be claimed where these relate to the project.

Costs of external training courses for staff can be claimed, again these must relate to the project.

2. Beneficiary costs - the following are eligible

Wages or a daily/weekly allowance paid to beneficiaries with National Insurance and pension where applicable.

Beneficiary daily travel costs and travel board and lodging for external courses.

Where you are paying for childcare (or other dependant care) rather than providing an in-house nursery or creche, you can claim the costs under this heading. For example, you may be planning to pay child minders or after school clubs.

3. *Other costs - the following are eligible*

Rent and leasing of buildings.

Hire and lease of equipment - operating leases only

Depreciation of owned equipment.

With effect from 1997 depreciation of premises can also be claimed

Purchase of consumables.

Purchase of small items of equipment to a maximum value of £350 per item. Please note that with effect from 1 May 1997 the purchase of second hand equipment is excluded from eligible expenditure costs.

Aids and minor adaptations of premises and equipment where the project will include people with disabilities, for example ramps, adaptations to toilets and computers.

The costs of external training courses for beneficiaries, for example college costs, first aid course.

Advertising of training courses.

Stationery, postage and telephone.

Rates/council tax, water rates, gas, electricity.

Insurance.

Basic office furnishings.

Cleaning, minor repairs and maintenance.

General documentation and administration costs incurred in support of ESF activity.

Running costs of any nursery provision where beneficiaries are not required to contribute to the costs.

Running costs of care of other dependants where beneficiaries do not contribute towards the costs.

Costs of the examination of the effectiveness of the training.

Costs of audit, legal and accountancy service where used for the ESF project.

For transnational projects you are able to claim translation and interpreting costs.

Where you are unable to reclaim VAT from HM Customs & Excise you can claim VAT costs that relate to the project

Eligible costs may differ for the different funds and in subsequent years, so it is vital that you check the current relevant guidance for the fund you are planning to apply under.

Ineligible expenditure

There are some costs that you cannot claim under an ESF project. These include:

Bank charges, loan interest, overdraft interest and other financial charges.

Consultancy fees, including any person or organisation you pay as a consultant to complete your ESF application and/or final claim forms, and management fees.

Non-statutory allowances paid to staff, including such things as commissions and profit sharing schemes.

Purchase of depreciable equipment and buildings, i.e. you can't claim for capital expenditure. However you can claim the depreciation costs of owned equipment, and remember you can buy individual items of equipment up to a limit of £350 cost per item.

Purchase of second hand equipment.

Appendix 1

APPENDIX 2

Examples of direct costs

Staff costs

You are planning a 10 week course for 8 beneficiaries at 21 hours (3 days) per week. You will be using an external trainer to deliver most of the training and have agreed one week's preparation time (5 days) initially with additionally 1 day a week preparation time besides the 3 days contact time with the trainees. The trainers charges are £250 per day plus VAT. You cannot reclaim the VAT from HM Customs and Excise.

The detail will be shown on the application form as follows:

External trainer 4 days a week for 10 weeks plus 5 days
preparation time – 45 days at £293.75 (incl VAT) £13,218.75

Beneficiary costs

You are planning to run a training course for 15 women returners over 13 weeks, 5 days a week, at 4 hours per day ie 20 hours per week. Experience has shown that on average two thirds of the women will require childcare for one child under five. The training will take place during the time that children over five years old are at school. You will be using child minders and expect to pay £2.50 per hour per child. Besides the 4 hours each day you allow an extra 1 hour travelling time per day (ie half an hour each way for the trainee travelling to and from the child minder).

The detail will be shown on the application form as follows:

Childcare costs for 10 under 5s for 13 weeks at 25 hours per
week at £2.50 per hour – 10 x 13 x 25 x £2.50 .. £8,125.00

Other costs

You are planning a project which includes training in three different skill areas, information technology skills, care skills and catering skills. You are planning to do some initial training in-house but will then contract with the local college for them to do the specific skills training to NVQ level 2. There will be 30 beneficiaries but until they are recruited you do not know how many will be interested in the three different skill areas. The college costs are £800 per person for the IT skills, £850 per person for the care skills and £825 per person for the catering skills. You could estimate the numbers you think there will be for each skill area, or you could take an average and use that figure to budget. The average cost of the courses are £825 per person.

The detail will be shown on the application form as follows:

College costs for 30 beneficiaries at an average cost of £825 per person £24,750

APPENDIX 3

Examples of apportionment based on staff time

Example 1

Your organisation employs 12 full time project staff plus a full time manager and one full time and one half time administrator. Holiday entitlement is 22 days per person plus 12 days public holidays per annum. The working week is 5 days, 37.5 hours.

Calculate the time each full time staff member is at work. This is:

Days worked in a year are 260 (52 weeks x 5 days) minus 34 days (annual plus public holidays) ie **226 days**. To calculate the hours worked, multiply by hours worked per day ie 7.5. This works out at **1695 hours** each person works in the year.

The calculate the total number of hours worked by project staff. This is 12 staff multiplied by 1695 hours per person, ie **20,340 hours**.

Then calculate the number of hours the project staff will spend on the ESF project.

Say this is a 26 week course with two groups of beneficiaries being trained at 18 hours per week each. One of the project staff will work on the project full time for the full 26 weeks with an additional 2 weeks preparation time. This is 28 weeks times 37.5 hours ie **1050 hours**. Two of the other project staff will work on the project, one doing 120 hours, the other doing 240 hours. **The total ESF project hours are therefore 1410.**

In order to calculate an overhead apportionment percentage divide the ESF project hours by the total project staff hours and multiply by 100.

$$\frac{1410}{20,340} \times 100 = 6.93\%$$

You can then use the overhead apportionment percentage to calculate the amounts of shared costs to charge to the project, including rent, rates, insurance and salaries of managers and other support staff.

Example 2

Your organisation employs three full time and one half time person. All are involved in project work and the administration tasks are shared. The working week is 5 days. The annual holiday entitlement is 25 days, public holidays are 11 days.

Days worked in a year are 260 (52 x 5) minus 36 days holiday ie **224 days per person**

The total number of staff days worked is 3.5 people multiplied by 224 days ie **784 days.**

The ESF project is running for 13 weeks at 3 days a week training and preparation. in addition to this there is a further 7 days preparation time built in plus 10 days for administration. All of the project staff have the necessary skills to do the training. There will only be one person at a time working on the project, ie training, doing the preparation, doing the admin. So the days to be spent on the project are as follows:

(13 weeks x 3 days) + 7 days prep + 10 days admin = **56 days**

In order to calculate the percentage of overheads to be charged to the ESF project divide the ESF project days by the total staff days and multiply by 100.

$$\frac{56}{784} \times 100 = 7.14\%$$

APPENDIX 4

Examples of apportionment based on beneficiary hours

Beneficiary hours are the hours spent by each beneficiary on the project. These hours can include training, guidance and counselling, work experience and home study. The training hours for each beneficiary must be recorded. The total beneficiary hours for an ESF project is the total of the actual hours of **each** beneficiary.

These are examples of apportionment to use at final claim stage and are based on actual hours not estimated hours.

Example 1

This project was for 20 beneficiaries, and in order to be eligible for this Objective and Pathway/Priority had to be unemployed for 6 months or longer. Although 20 eligible beneficiaries were recruited 5 left early as they managed to find permanent employment. The organisation decided to recruit 5 more beneficiaries to bring the numbers back up to 20 but all of the 5 had been unemployed for less than 6 months so were ineligible for the ESF project. The 15 remaining ESF eligible beneficiaries and the 5 non ESF eligible trainees then went on to complete the training. The full course was 400 hours per beneficiary.

The actual training hours were as follows:

The 15 ESF *eligible* trainees who started and completed the course did **5,873 hours.** These figures were actuals and were taken from trainee time sheets.

The 5 ESF *eligible* trainees who started but left early did **1112 hours.** Again these were actuals taken from time sheets.

The 5 ESF *ineligible* trainees who started part way through the course and went on to complete the training did an actual **1217 hours.**

The total ESF hours are therefore 5873 plus 1112, ie **6985 hours.**

The total trainee hours spent on the project are 5873 plus 1112 plus 1217, ie **8202 hours.**

In order to calculate the total project costs that can be allocated to the ESF project,

$$\frac{6985}{8202} \times 100 = \textbf{85.16\%}$$

Example 2

Because ESF administration is so precise and time-consuming, you may decide to employ an ESF administration worker who is dedicated to keeping ESF records for the projects you are running. The costs of the worker can then be divided between the projects using a formula based on beneficiary hours.

Assuming the cost of the worker was £9,775.

Three ESF projects were run during the year. The actual beneficiary hours (taken from completed time sheets were as follows:

Project A – 6,900 hours

Project B – 10,300 hours

Project C – 1,945 hours

Total hours for all three projects are 19,145 hours.

The cost of the administration worker is apportioned as follows:

Project A $\frac{6,900}{19,145} \times £9,775 = £3,522.98$

Project B $\frac{10,300}{19,145} \times £9,775 = £5,258.95$

Project C $\frac{1,945}{19,145} \times £9,775 = £993.07$

APPENDIX 5

Example of apportionment based on space/ area

Example

An ESF project is running for 6 months from July to December. The project promoters have decided to apportion the rent and rates, heat and light, cleaning and building insurance by area used. The trainees are to be trained on the premises for 21 hours per week. The normal week is 35 hours. The organisation occupies a building with 3,000 square foot of space. The training project will use 500 square foot of space.

If the rent and rates are £12,000 for the whole organisation for the full year, then the calculation on the application form would be as follows:

Rent/rates £12,000 – 500 sq ft used out of a total of 3,000 sq ft for

six months for 21 hours per week.

$$£12,000 \times \frac{500}{3,000} \times \frac{1}{2} \text{ year} \times \frac{21}{35} \text{ hours} = £600$$

APPENDIX 6

An example of the wording that may be used in a letter from a public match funder who is providing matching funding in-kind.

The letter must be on the official letter head of the public match funder and must be addressed to the organisation in receipt of the in-kind match funding and the ESF monies. It must be signed by an officer of the public match funder.

> *"This is to confirm that this organisation has provided public matching funding in-kind for ESF project reference (insert ESF dossier number and project letter) and that the actual in-kind costs are as follows:*

Other costs

> *Créche places provided free of charge to ESF beneficiaries, the running costs of the crêche per hour per child is £1.25 per hour.*

> *Costs were for 17 children at an average per child of 325 hours at £1.25 per hour*

> $$17 \times 325 \times £1.25 = £6906.25$$

> *Full attendance records are available for all the children attending the créche.*

> *Total in-kind match funding provided is £6906.25*

> *A Public Match Funding Certificate will be provided for this amount.*

> *We confirm that there is full documentation available to back up all costs incurred and that this will be available for examination at an ESF verification visit".*

APPENDIX 7

This is an example of a schedule or spreadsheet you can use to analyse the direct costs of your ESF project.
The date column is used for the invoice date. The detail column is used to note what the expenditure was for. The supplier column is for you to note the supplier of the goods or services. The reference column is very important and is there for you to put in the reference number/letter so that the original documentation for each entry is easily retrievable within the filing system of your organisation.

The value of the invoice or petty cash voucher is then entered in the "Total" column and entered again in the relevant expenditure column. The expenditure columns should be labelled with the costs that you included in your application form.

Each month the total of the "Total" column should equal the figure shown as direct project costs for this project as shown in your organisation's main books of account. The sum of all of the amounts in the different costs columns should equal the figure in the total column.

The example shows details of the direct costs of a project that started on 1st April. The figures are cumulative, ie at the end of May, the total costs shown are for April and May.

When you are preparing your final claim forms for ESF the total of each cost column is the one you use in the final claim for each of the direct costs. The total equals the figure for the direct costs of the project as shown in the organisation's main financial records. An auditor could easily check any particular invoices because there is a reference shown for each one. The schedule itself will be part of the back-up documentation you keep to show how the final claim was put together.

ESF Direct Costs 1997

Dossier No. 979999 UK3 Project A

Date	Detail	Supplier	Ref	Total	Trainee Travel	Childcare Costs	Staff Travel subsistance	Consumables	Advertising
1 April	Advertising	Courier	97/207	57.00					57.00
2 April	Leaflet printing	Sealion Print	97/210	150.00					150.00
8 April	Leaflet Distrib.	J. Brown	97/211	16.50			16.50		
April Sub Total				**223.50**			**16.50**		**207.00**
19 May	Trainee Travel Exp	Trainees	PC 70-85	173.20	173.20				
19 May	Childcare	BB Nursery	97/376	97.30		97.30			
19 May	Childcare	P Stone	97/377	45.00		45.00			
19 May	Childcare	M Davey	97/378	45.00		45.00			
20 May	Training Materials	Jaycee UK	97/381	227.35				227.35	
27 May	Trainee Travel Exp	Trainees	PC 110-123	167.25	167.25				
27 May	Childcare	BB Nursery	97/402	97.30		97.30			
27 May	Childcare	P Stone	97/403	45.00		45.00			
30 May	Childcare	M Davey	97/405	45.00		45.00			
May Sub Total				**1165.90**	**340.45**	**374.60**	**16.50**	**227.35**	**207.00**

NB The total for each month should agree with the total in the main financial records of the organisation. The total of each column added together should agree with the total of the total column in each period.

APPENDIX 8

This is an example of how you could set out a monthly salary schedule to charge the salary costs to different ESF projects and to non ESF activity.
The staff column shows the name of the individual member of staff. The hours in the month is the number of hours they were each at work. The total cost of each staff member is divided into gross salary, Employers' National Insurance Contribution (NIC) and pension costs. There are two ESF projects, A and B. Non ESF activity has to be included in order to make the figures balance.

The column labelled "Proj A s/hours" is for the staff hours worked on Project A by each staff member in the month. Similarly there are columns of the staff hours spent on Project B and on non ESF work. The ESF project cost for "J BROWN" for project A for the month is calculated by dividing her salary (and Employers' NIC and pension costs) by the total number of hours worked in the month, and multiplying by the number of hours worked on project A.

J BROWN's salary £1,250.00 —140 hours x 100 hours = £892.86 cost to project A

Each of the analysed costs are calculated in a similar way ie by dividing the total cost by the total number of hours worked per person, then multiplying by the number of hours worked on the individual project.

This schedule shows the costs for one month only. You would need to combine the total for each month in order to find the cumulative totals to date. The total costs of salaries, including Employers' NIC and pension costs should equal the costs shown in the organisation's main financial records.

You should take the staff hours worked on the project from time sheets for the month.

You don't have to do this on a monthly basis; you could do it every two or three months if you wish. The schedule would be part of the working papers for the completion of the ESF final claim forms.

ESF Apportioned salary costs 1997

Dossier No 979999UK3
*NB all details from payroll records - this is agreed with
the ledger each month*

Month May 1997

Staff	Hours in month		Total	Proj A s/hours	Proj A cost	Proj B s/hours	Proj B cost	Non ESF s/hours	Non ESF cost
J BROWN	140	Salary	1250.00	100	892.86	40	357.14	0	0.00
		Empl'ers NIC	127.60		91.14		36.46		
		Pension	62.50		44.64		17.86		
L BEE	140	Salary	1250.00	20	178.57	120	1071.43	0	0.00
		Empl'ers NIC	127.60		18.22		109.38		
		Pension	62.50		8.93		53.57		
M PRASAD	140	Salary	1250.00	20	178.57	100	892.86	20	178.57
		Empl'ers NIC	127.60		18.22		91.16		18.22
		Pension	62.50		8.93		44.64		8.93
S KEELEY	140	Salary	1000.00	0	0.00	115	821.43	25	178.57
		Empl'ers NIC	101.90				83.70		18.20
		Pension	50.00				40.78		9.22
S BALA	140	Salary	1000.00	0	0.00	0	0.00	140	1000.00
		Empl'ers NIC	101.90						101.90
		Pension	50.00						50.00
TOTALS	**700**		**6624.10**	**140**	**1440.08**	**375**	**3620.41**	**185**	**1563.61**

*NB The totals for each month can then be transferred to another analysis
sheet or you can slot in the brought forward figure under the totals for
the month, add them to the month's totals and you have a cumulative
figure to date.*

APPENDIX 9

Example of how to calculate depreciation if your organisation has a different financial year from the ESF year of January to December.

Your organisation's financial year runs from 1st April to 31st March. You have run an ESF funded computer training project from January 1st to September 30th 1998 and are now preparing the final claim information. Your organisation's depreciation policy is to depreciate computer equipment on a straight line basis over four years. You do not allow for residual values.

Your last set of published accounts for the period up to the end of March 1998 shows the following detail for depreciation. This is for the period April 1997 to March 1998.

To continue the example, the published accounts for the last financial year show a depreciation cost for computers of £3,975.00. If you calculate a quarter of this charge, it will give you the depreciation costs for the period January to March 1998. **This is £993.75.**

In order to calculate the depreciation costs for the period following the 31st March 1998, you will need to look at your current fixed asset register. Check to see which items of computer equipment have been fully depreciated and ignore those. List the items of equipment that still have some value and add any new items purchased since the end of the last financial year.

For the example, there are fixed assets with some value of £12,100 plus new items were purchased to a value of £5,500. Total value of fixed assets (computer equipment) to be depreciated are £17,600 (£12,100 + £5,500). The depreciation costs for the year (April 1998 to March 1999) are then calculated at 25% of the current value of the fixed assets.

This is £4,400 i.e. £17,600 at 25%. You then need to further break down this figure to find the cost for the period April to September 1998 (remember the ESF project finished at the end of September). This is six months, so calculate half of the £4,400 for the period i.e. **£2,200.**

Add the costs of the two periods, January to March **£993.75** and April to September **£2,200.00**, and you have the depreciation cost for the period January to September i.e. **£3,193.75.**

You will then need to apportion the figure of £3,193.75 in order to reflect the use of the computer equipment by the ESF project, for example if all of the equipment were used half of the time for the project, then you would charge half of £3,193.75 to the ESF project costs i.e. £1,596.87. The usage of the equipment for ESF purposes has to be supported by documentation.